SIMPLY YUNNAN

Simple Ingredients,
Simple Technique

Less time in the kitchen,
More time around
the table.

REBECCA D.
HENDERSON

www.rebeccadiann.com
rebeccadiann@pobox.com

ISBN-13: 978-1481287791
ISBN-10: 1481287796

Cover design and formatting by Streetlight Graphics

Dedication
For Stephen

TABLE OF CONTENTS

INTRODUCTION

I love Yunnan food, and I love simple recipes.

Ten years of eating in Yunnan led to this cookbook. I want to share the simple recipes I've collected from friends and from trial-and-error recreating dishes from favorite restaurants. These are the dishes I cook to remind myself of towns where I lived, of people I miss — to remind me of places and moments wrapped up in flavors and textures.

The cuisine of Yunnan is often overlooked in favor of the foods of other more popular regions of China — Beijing duck, dumplings of the northeast, wheat noodles from the north, rich and complex flavors from Cantonese areas, and the heat of Sichuan chilies. Though Yunnan has long been one of the most popular travel destinations in China for both Chinese and foreign tourists alike and its unique foods feature prominently in the memories of visitors to the area, most Chinese cookbooks fail to pay substantial homage to the region. It's a shame, really, for Yunnan's cuisine deserves more attention, and Westerners could use a handy resource for recreating at home the dishes so popular in Yunnan.

A lover of Chinese food for many years, I've found Chinese cookbooks are often complicated and exotic, the recipes inaccessible to someone who 1) has limited time to cook and 2) lives in an area that doesn't have a Chinatown with large Asian grocery stores. The photos in these cookbooks make my mouth water, but the list of ingredients and the methods involved in preparing the dishes keep me from trying out new recipes. Sometimes I think it would be easier to buy a plane ticket and head to Shanghai for dinner than to attempt gathering the ingredients for some of the recipes I've read.

My desire for this book is to share *simple* recipes that don't have surprise ingredients or complicated instructions requiring excessive amounts of time or energy. In general I left recipes out of this collection that call for unreasonable ingredients, but in instances where a recipe needs something unique, I provide tips for where to find the ingredient or a reasonable substitute to simplify your shopping and cooking experiences. My hope is that you'll find you can easily cook these recipes with ingredients readily available in the West.

I made this commitment to simplicity in Yunnan cooking, simplicity both in ingredients and in technique, out of a desire that we all have more time to enjoy the most important elements of a meal. Less stress in food preparation means more time and energy to enjoy sitting down to a meal with loved ones to bond over food. Many a friend was made over bowls of rice or noodles during my time in Yunnan, and I pray these recipes give you opportunity to deepen relationships of your own.

YUNNAN – SOUTH OF THE CLOUDS

Yunnan — "South of the Clouds" in Chinese — is home to twenty-five of the officially recognized ethnic minorities in China. Ethnic tourism is a huge draw for the province, with Chinese and foreign tourists alike flocking to the southwest corner of China to experience the colorful costumes, lively music, and mysterious festivals of the various people groups. The languages and traditions of the peoples vary widely, from the Tibetans, Naxi, and Bai of northern Yunnan to the Dai, Bulang, and Wa of the south.

The cuisine of Yunnan is equally as eclectic as the languages and customs of its peoples. In a few meals in the provincial capital of Kunming you can taste flavors representing the styles of East, Southeast, South, and Central Asia, all in restaurants located along the same street. The lime and cilantro of Southeast Asia meets the sour and spicy combination popular in Southwest China.

One remarkable difference in Yunnan cuisine from that in other parts of China is the use of rice noodles instead of wheat. Thin, round, flat, broad, boiled, fried — the people of Yunnan love their rice noodles in all shapes, sizes, and forms and at all times of the day. It took me a year or two, but I eventually became accustomed to the Yunnan habit of eating a bowl of rice noodles in a meat broth for breakfast. A far cry from the toast and oatmeal I grew up eating each morning, but sitting on a short stool on the sidewalk with countless other *Yunnanren* eating our noodle breakfast was a great way to embrace the local culture and make new friends.

I was fortunate enough during my ten years in Yunnan to travel widely throughout the province, after an initial two years living and studying Mandarin in Kunming. The majority of my time in Yunnan, however, was spent in the southern areas along the borders of Burma and Laos, areas where the ethnic groups favor Burmese, Lao, and Thai traditions and cuisine over Han Chinese or Tibetan. As a result, several of the dishes I've included in this collection are unique to the people groups living in the southern border areas. I'm not intentionally leaving out groups like the Yi, Naxi, Bai, or Tibetans from this cookbook, except that my experience eating their foods is more limited than my experience with groups like the Dai, Bulang, and Wa — and my cooking experience for the northern groups is more limited still.

APPRECIATING THE NOT–SO–SIMPLE

Though my cookbook strives to maintain an attitude of simplicity in ingredients and methods, many of the dishes I ate over the years in Yunnan were far from simple in any aspect. Some dishes included ingredients only found in certain remote locations at certain times of the year, making me feel overwhelmingly welcomed when a local family shared the treasured dish with me, an outsider. Other dishes took hours (or days!) to prepare, meats simmering over low heat to achieve the perfect tenderness and complexity of flavors. In writing a cookbook of simple recipes, these unique local dishes had to be excluded, but I want my appreciation on the record in favor of the exotic, not just the simple, in Yunnan cuisine. It's not that I don't love the exotic; it's just that I can't replicate it at home in the West.

It's impossible to replicate an omelet made of eggs steamed with a nest of rice paddy ants found only during the season when the rice seedlings are transplanted from the seed bed to the fields. My friend Guiying served this remarkable dish to me and my friends after a day of hiking on a mountain outside the predominantly Dai city of Mangshi. The eggs were cooked to perfection, melt-in-your-mouth delicious, and the ants added a hint of spiciness with hardly even an extra crunch. Once I got over the psychological effect of eating insects, I was honored that Guiying's family would share this once-a-year treat with us.

In a Bulang village on another stretch of the China-Burma border, I enjoyed for the first time *niu pa fu*, a savory stew of beef, mint, and chilies served over steamed rice. I first heard of *niu pa fu* from my friend Lydia, whose mother ran a noodle shop and restaurant out of their home — her *niu pa fu* was famous throughout the local area and would sell out quickly to travelers on market day.

Lydia's mother also served me many bowls of a breakfast dish of eggs poached in brown sugar and partially fermented rice (it sounds horrid, but don't knock it till you've tried it). I took my own mother to visit Lydia's mom at her village restaurant, where she served us a pot of soup made from what I call "chainsaw chicken" — an entire freshly butchered chicken cut into bite-size pieces using a cleaver, meat and bones and organs and all in one large pot with herbs and spices. The meat can be hard to eat off the tiny pieces of bone, but the flavor of the soup's fresh chicken broth is heavenly. I would love to recreate the broth in my own kitchen, but alas, it would be impossible to find all the ingredients, nor do I have the upper body strength to hack apart a chicken with a cleaver the way Lydia's mom can.

If you've traveled in Yunnan, I'm sure you have food memories similar to my own, and maybe this book will cause you to wax nostalgic over meals shared with friends or strangers. If you haven't had the good fortune of visiting Yunnan, I hope you can try a few of these simple recipes and experience the flavors of this province.

HOW TO GET THE MOST
FROM THIS BOOK

I've grouped the recipes into four categories: Rice and Noodles; Soups; Meat and Fish; Vegetables and Fruits. Every recipe in this book is made "Yunnan style;" you may see similar dishes in other parts of China, but these recipes replicate the way I experienced these foods while in Yunnan.

Because of the preference of rice over wheat in Yunnan, all but two of the recipes in this book can be prepared as gluten-free with the simple substitution of gluten-free soy sauce, available in most grocery stores.

You'll find the following abbreviations next to recipe names in the list:

S = Extra simple recipe that requires little time and few ingredients
V = Vegetarian
F = Includes wheat flour

Throughout the book I have indicated that many dishes are to be cooked using oil, typically a small amount for stir-frying. Most households and restaurants in Yunnan commonly use canola oil. However, if you are conscientious about using less-refined oils in your diet, feel free to substitute coconut oil in stir-fry dishes or olive oil in dishes cooked with lower heat.

I've also included ideas for which dishes to serve together, along with hints for shopping or preparation, including tips for where to find ingredients, easy substitutions, and time-saving tactics.

Now, time to start cooking and then, as they say in Yunnan, *man man chi* — slowly slowly eat. Savor time with family and friends as you enjoy these simple dishes together!

LIST OF RECIPES

NOODLES AND RICE

Rice Noodle Soup
Fried Flat Rice Noodles
Fried Rice with Fried Peanuts
Ham-and-Potato Rice (S)
Pork-and-Turnip Rice
· Sticky Rice
Pineapple Sticky Rice

SOUPS

Pork Ribs Soup 一 (Cabbage and Tofu)
Pork Ribs Soup 二 (Turnips)
Clear Broth Fish Soup (S)
Autumn Soup (V)

MEAT AND FISH

Fish Steamed with Herbs and Spices
Pork and Peppers
Pork in Banana Leaf
Ham and Soybeans with Goat Cheese

VEGETABLES AND FRUITS

Pickled Turnips (V)
Pickled Greens (V)
Cucumber Salad (S, V)
Green Beans with Garlic (V)
Stir-fried Cabbage (S, V)
Corn fried with Green and Red Peppers (S, V)
Crispy Beans with Pickled Greens (S, V, F)

Tofu with Green Onions and Tomato (S, V)
Grandma Potatoes (V)
Crispy Yunnan Hashbrowns (V)
Spicy Sweet Eggplant (V)
Roasted Eggplant (V)
Roasted Tomato Dip (V)
Fried Bananas (V, F)
Xishuangbanna Limeade (V)

S = Extra simple recipe that requires little time and few ingredients
V = Vegetarian
F = Includes wheat flour

NOODLES AND RICE

RICE NOODLE SOUP

Rice noodles in soup is without a doubt the most common meal served throughout Yunnan — suitable for breakfast, lunch, dinner, or a midnight snack. Each region of the province has its own special way of preparing the soup, with the people from each area declaring their local version the absolute best to be found in Yunnan. Whatever type of stock you use for a base, whatever type of meat you decide to use as the accompaniment, just add a dash of soy sauce and vinegar, a spoonful of chopped green onions, a few sprigs of cilantro, and some crushed red pepper flakes to give the soup the finishing touches to suit your own taste.

Serves 4
Prep time: 5 minutes
Cooking time: 35 minutes

- chopped cilantro, red pepper flakes, soy sauce (regular or gluten-free), and vinegar for seasoning

- 10 c. beef or chicken stock
- 1-inch piece of ginger, peeled and crushed with the flat side of a cleaver blade
- 3 whole star anise
- 2 whole cloves
- 1 to 1 1/2 c. cooked meat (beef or chicken, depending on which type of stock you use), thinly sliced
- 1 c. cabbage or spinach, cut in 2-inch pieces
- 2 green onions, cut in 1-inch strips
- 10 c. water
- 12 oz. rice noodles (usually labeled as "rice stick" or "rice vermicelli")
- salt to taste

In a large stock pot, bring the meat stock to a boil over medium-high heat, along with the ginger, star anise, cloves, and meat slices. Reduce heat and simmer for 30 minutes. Remove the ginger, star anise, and cloves from the soup. Add the cabbage or spinach and green onions and simmer for 3 minutes.

During the final 10 minutes of cooking the soup, prepare the rice noodles. In a large pot, bring 10 c. water to a boil over medium-high heat. Add the rice noodles, reduce heat to medium, and boil the noodles for 4 to 5 minutes. Remove the pot from the heat and allow the noodles to continue soaking in the hot water for another 4 to 5 minutes. Alternatively, prepare the noodles according to the package's instructions. Drain the water from the noodles.

Divide the cooked noodles evenly into 4 large soup bowls. Ladle equal amounts of soup with meat, onions, and leafy vegetables over the noodles in each bowl. Allow each person to add cilantro, red pepper flakes, soy sauce, and vinegar according to his or her own taste.

Shopping note:

This noodle soup is best prepared using a type of thin, round rice noodle usually labeled in English as "rice stick" or "rice vermicelli" and found at Asian markets or on the Asian aisle at your grocery store.

Preparation note:

Plan to make this soup when you have leftover cooked meat that you can thinly slice; choose to make the soup with beef or chicken stock according to the type of meat you have leftover.

FRIED FLAT RICE NOODLES

Rice noodles and other foods made with rice flour are a staple in Yunnan. City streets near residential and business areas are often lined with noodle shops serving up a quick plate or bowl to hurried eaters at all hours of the day. Fried noodle or rice dishes in Yunnan street restaurants tend to be heavy on oil, salt, and MSG, but adapting them for home cooking produces a flavorful, healthy, gluten-free dish that gives the street cooks a run for their money.

Serves 2 as a main dish, more as a side dish
Prep time: 10 to 15 minutes
Cooking time: 5 minutes

- 8 c. water
- 8 oz. package of wide, flat rice noodles (sometimes labeled "rice flakes")
- 1 Tbsp oil
- 2 cloves garlic, minced
- 1 dried red pepper, sliced in half lengthwise, seeds removed
- 1 c. cured ham, thinly sliced and cut in 1-inch pieces
- 2 c. cabbage, chopped in 1-inch pieces
- 1 small tomato, cut in 1-inch slices
- 1 Tbsp soy sauce (regular or gluten-free)
- 2 green onions, cut in 1-inch strips

In a large pot, bring 8 c. water to a boil. Remove from heat and add the rice noodles to soak for 10 minutes, until tender. Alternatively, prepare the noodles according to the package's instructions. Drain the water from the noodles.

Heat the oil in a wok over medium-high heat. Fry the garlic and dried pepper for 1 minute. Add the noodles, ham, cabbage, tomato, and soy sauce; stir-fry for 2 to 3 minutes until the cabbage is wilted and the noodles are coated with soy sauce. Add the green onions and stir-fry for 1 minute. Serve hot.

Shopping note:

This fried noodle dish is best prepared using a type of wide, flat rice noodle usually labeled in English as "rice flakes" and found at Asian markets or on the Asian aisle at your grocery store.

Most cooks in Yunnan use a local variation of salty, cured ham called (surprise) Yunnan ham. If you're cooking in a Western context, you can substitute cured ham, preferably without honey flavoring.

If your grocery store doesn't have dried red peppers in their Asian food section, check the Hispanic food aisle for whole dried Japanese peppers (*chili japones entero*).

Preparation note:

To make the most efficient use of your time, you can cut up your ham and vegetables while the noodles are soaking.

FRIED RICE WITH FRIED PEANUTS

It's tempting to ask why I bothered including a fried rice recipe in this collection — the dish is a standard for Asian cookbooks, and recipes abound. But this version has a distinctly Yunnanese flair, and as soon as I put one bite in my mouth, it reminds me of countless meals eaten in roadside shops. If you're stuck in a fried rice rut, this recipe is definitely worth a try. The fried peanuts served on the side add a nice crunchiness to balance the textures of rice, pork, and vegetables — plus, you gain valuable practice on your chopsticks technique by picking up each individual nut. You wanted that practice, right?

Serves 4 as a main dish, more as a side dish
Prep time: 10 minutes
Cooking time: 15 minutes (25 including peanuts)

- 1 lb. ground pork
- 2 dried red peppers, sliced in half lengthwise, seeds removed
- 3 to 4 green onions, chopped
- 3 c. cooked rice
- salt to taste
- 2 c. chopped leafy green vegetable (lettuce, cabbage, kale, collard greens, or whatever greens you have on hand) OR 3/4 c. pickled vegetables (see recipe for **Pickled Greens** in the **Vegetables and Fruits** section)

In a large wok, cook the ground pork over medium-high heat until browned through, being careful to break up the clumps with your stir-fry utensil. Drain excess fat, leaving behind enough to coat the wok and keep the rice from sticking. Add the dried peppers and green onions; fry for 1 minute. Add the rice and salt, stirring well to mix the ingredients and heat the rice thoroughly. Stir in the chopped greens and fry until wilted. Serve warm, with fried peanuts on the side.

The bright color of the dried red peppers adds aesthetic appeal to your final presentation, but be sure to inform your guests not to eat them — or do so at their own peril.

Fried Peanuts

- 6 to 8 Tbsp oil (enough to form a thin layer over the bottom of the wok)
- 2 c. raw red-skinned peanuts, with skins
- salt to taste

Heat the oil in a wok over medium-high heat. Add the peanuts and fry until crispy (about 7 to 8 minutes). Spoon the peanuts onto a towel-covered plate to drain the oil, and sprinkle with salt to your desired taste.

Shopping note:

Check the bulk food section of your grocery store for raw peanuts with skins. If your grocery store doesn't have dried red peppers in their Asian food section, check the Hispanic food aisle for whole dried Japanese peppers (*chili japones entero*).

HAM–AND–POTATO RICE

During my first year living in Yunnan, I spent every Sunday evening at a friend's house for a few hours of language exchange — she would practice English, I would practice Chinese. Her mother cooked us dinner every week, and her Ham-and-Potato Rice became comfort food for me, mainly because it was a local dish I could enjoy without subjecting my palate to intense chilies! The ingredients are simple, yet the meal is flavorful because of the ham. Soybeans or peas can give it some added variety, and **Stir-fried Cabbage** on the side provides another serving of veggies to your daily diet.

Serves 4 to 6

Prep time: 10 minutes

Cooking time: Varies according to rice cooker; 20 to 25 minutes on stove top

- 3/4 c. cured ham, diced
- 1 small potato (about 3/4 c.), peeled and diced
- 1/2 c. green peas or soybeans (optional), fresh or frozen, shelled
- 1 1/2 c. uncooked rice
- 1/2 tsp salt
- If using a rice cooker, 2 c. water
- If cooking on the stove top, 3 c. water

Rice Cooker Instructions:

Place diced ham, potato, peas or soybeans (optional), and rice in the pot of a rice cooker. Add water and salt, and stir 3 or 4 times to distribute salt. Cook according to your rice cooker instructions. Serve in rice bowls with **Stir-fried Cabbage** and a soup (such as **Clear Broth Fish Soup**) on the side.

Stove Top Instructions:

Place diced ham, potato, peas or soybeans (optional), and rice in a medium pot. Add water and salt, and stir 3 or 4 times to distribute the salt. Bring the water to a boil; reduce heat to low and cover. Simmer for 20 to 25 minutes, until the water is absorbed and the rice is done.

Shopping note:

Most cooks in Yunnan use a local variation of salty, cured ham called (surprise) Yunnan ham. If you're cooking in a Western context, you can substitute cured ham, preferably without honey flavoring.

PORK–AND–TURNIP RICE

When I lived in Yunnan I often wanted something quick, inexpensive, and delicious to eat for lunch — but it was easy to become tired of fried rice. A common alternative to fried rice is *gai fan,* or "covered rice," where a plate of steamed rice is served covered in a thick sauce. The **Pickled Turnips** of this pork-and-turnip version of "covered rice" give the dish a distinctly Yunnan tang.

Serves 2 as a main dish, more as a side dish
Prep time: 10 minutes
Cooking time: 5 minutes

- 1 Tbsp oil
- 2 cloves garlic, minced
- 1/2 c. **Pickled Turnips** (see recipe in the **Vegetables and Fruits** section), diced
- 1/2 c. red bell pepper, diced
- 1/2 lb. ground pork
- 1/4 tsp salt
- steamed rice

Heat the oil in a wok over medium-high heat. When the oil is hot, add the garlic, pickled turnips, and red bell pepper, and stir-fry for 1 minute. Add the ground pork and salt, and stir-fry until the pork is thoroughly cooked, about 3 to 4 minutes, being careful to break up the clumps of ground pork with your stir-fry utensil. Drain the excess fat. Serve the pork-and-turnip mixture over steamed rice.

26

STICKY RICE

More so than regular steamed rice, sticky rice is a distinctly Southeast Asian staple. In villages in southern Yunnan sticky rice accompanies meat and vegetables at regular meals, is dished out in large quantities for wedding banquets, or sweetened with sugar, fruit, and nuts to make special treats. While living in Jinghong, my favorite local breakfast was sticky rice, barbecue pork, and pickled vegetables, purchased from Dai ladies in my local market or along the street.

Serves 4 to 6
Prep time: 30 minutes to soak rice
Cooking time: 10 minutes

- 1 c. sticky rice, uncooked
- 2 c. water
- Soak the rice in the water for 30 minutes in a large glass bowl. Drain off 3/4 c. of the water, leaving the rice covered by 1/4 inch of water.

Shopping note:
Sticky rice is typically available at Asian markets and may also be labeled as *glutinous rice*.

Place the rice in a microwave oven, cover, and cook on *high* until the water is mostly absorbed but the rice is still wet, about 8 minutes; stir and cook until almost dry, an additional 1 1/2 to 2 minutes. Handle the bowl and lid carefully when removing it from the microwave — both will be hot, and the rice will create a lot of steam that can burn.

PINEAPPLE STICKY RICE

From my earliest days living in the provincial capital, Kunming, and visiting Dai restaurants with friends as a treat, Pineapple Sticky Rice has been a personal favorite. Sweet, fruity, and served in a hollowed out pineapple, it's hard to say if this sticky rice dish is a regular side dish or a dessert. After years of enjoying it, a Dai friend in Xishuangbanna taught me the "secret" of pineapple sticky rice — the secret is there are only four ingredients and a little time standing between you and this unique goodie.

Serves 6 to 8

Prep time: 30 minutes to soak rice; 10 to 15 minutes to cut pineapple; 2 minutes to mix

Cooking time: 10 minutes for rice; 1 minute to heat pineapple

- 1 pineapple (2 1/2 c. fresh pineapple, chopped); or 1 20 oz. can of crushed pineapple, drained well
- 1/3 c. sugar
- 1 c. **Sticky Rice**, uncooked
- 2 c. water

If you're using a fresh pineapple, refer to the photo for hollowing out the inside of the pineapple. Cut the spikes from the top of the pineapple and discard. Carefully slice off the top of the pineapple in one 1/2- to 1- inch thick piece, and set the slice aside — this will become the "lid" of your dish later. To hollow out your pineapple "bowl," work your knife around the inside of the pineapple about 1/4 inch from the outer edge, and loosen the flesh. One way to more easily remove the pineapple flesh is to divide the pineapple into quadrants, making a large X with the knife in the center of the pineapple. From here you can focus on cutting out the flesh one quadrant at a time, taking care not to slice through the outer layer. The bottom layer of your pineapple "bowl" will be thicker than the side layers — you'll know to stop cutting when the fruit becomes tougher and more difficult to remove.

Once all of the flesh has been removed, chop the fruit into small pieces and set aside. Drain any excess juice from your pineapple "bowl" —

I like to drain it into a cup and drink the fresh juice immediately.

If you're using canned pineapple, be sure to drain the juice thoroughly, in order to allow the sticky rice to maintain the correct consistency once the fruit and rice are mixed.

Prepare the **Sticky Rice** according to the instructions on the previous pages. Mix the chopped pineapple, sugar, and sticky rice in a bowl, taking care not to burn yourself with the hot rice or the steam.

If you're using canned pineapple, transfer the sticky rice mixture to a medium glass bowl.

If you're using a fresh pineapple, fill your pineapple "bowl" with the sticky rice mixture, packing the rice in. Replace the top "lid" on the pineapple. Depending on how much fruit you removed from the pineapple, you may have extra sticky rice mixture left over; the extra can be saved in a separate container to eat later or to refill your pineapple "bowl" during the meal.

Before serving, heat the pineapple sticky rice (whether in a glass bowl or your pineapple "bowl") on *high* for 30 seconds to 1 minute in the microwave.

Shopping notes:

Sticky rice is typically available at Asian markets and may also be labeled as *glutinous rice*.

If you're able to find a fresh pineapple for a reasonable price per pound and you have the time to cut up the fruit, it's worth it to use fresh fruit and serve it in the pineapple bowl to give your meal a festive, tropical vibe. If not, canned pineapple makes just as tasty a dish.

Preparation notes:

Americans tend to throw away the tough inner core of the pineapple and only eat the softer flesh, but in this dish I prefer to stick to the Asian method of eating all the flesh, core and all. The pineapple should be chopped finely enough that you won't be able to tell which pieces are from the core and which aren't — and you're able to get more fruit out of one pineapple!

The Dai people traditionally steam the pineapple rice mixture in the pineapple "bowl" just long enough to make sure all the fruit is heated through. If you have a large steamer (like those used for tamales), you may prefer to use the traditional method rather than a microwave, steaming for 5 minutes. I, however, find the microwave works just fine and is much simpler.

SOUPS

PORK RIBS SOUP
— (CABBAGE AND TOFU)

The simple, flavorful broth of Pork Ribs Soup works perfectly as a side to **Fried Rice** or with a meal of steamed rice and vegetable dishes. I learned to make the first version (一, or *yi*, for "one") with cabbage and tofu after eating it at a friend's house, while the second version (二, or *er*, for "two") with turnips was a popular side dish at a restaurant my friends and I frequented in the town of Mangshi. Both are worth trying — buy a pound of pork ribs, split it in half, and freeze a portion for later.

Serves 4 to 6 in a family-style meal
Prep time: 5 minutes
Cooking time: 35 minutes

- 1/2 lb. pork ribs, separated, cut into thirds (making rib pieces about 1 1/2 inches long)
- 8 c. water
- 8 oz. firm tofu, cut in 1-inch cubes
- 1 1/2 tsp salt
- 3 c. cabbage, chopped in 2-inch pieces

Place the ribs and water in a large pot, and bring to a boil over medium-high heat. Lower the heat to medium and boil for 30 minutes, until the meat is no longer pink in the middle.

Add the tofu and salt and boil for 2 minutes. Add the cabbage and boil until it is slightly wilted and bright green, about 3 minutes. Serve as a side dish to a meal with fried rice or steamed rice.

Shopping note:

Ask the butcher at your grocery store to cut the pork ribs into thirds, sparing yourself and your knife the effort.

PORK RIBS SOUP (TURNIPS)

Serves 4 to 6 in a family-style meal
Prep time: 5 minutes
Cooking time: 35 minutes

- 1/2 lb. pork ribs, separated, cut into thirds (making rib pieces about 1 1/2 inches long)
- 8 c. water
- 2 c. turnips (about 1 or 2 turnips), washed, peeled, and cut in 1-inch pieces
- 1 1/2 tsp salt

Place the ribs and water in a large pot, and bring to a boil over medium-high heat. Lower the heat to medium and boil for 30 minutes, until the meat is no longer pink in the middle.

Add the turnip pieces and salt, and boil for 5 minutes, until tender. Serve as a side dish to a meal with fried rice or steamed rice.

Shopping note:

Ask the butcher at your grocery store to cut the pork ribs into thirds, sparing yourself and your knife the effort.

CLEAR BROTH FISH SOUP

As simple as it gets. This light recipe came from my friend Lydia and makes a wonderful accompaniment to steamed rice and stir-fried dishes.

Serves 4 to 6 in a family-style meal
Prep time: 5 minutes
Cooking time: 7 minutes

- 3 frozen tilapia fillets, thawed and cut in 2-inch pieces
- 6 c. water
- 1 tsp salt
- 1/4 c. cilantro, chopped
- 6 green onions, cut into 3-inch slices
- 1-inch piece of ginger, peeled

Place the tilapia fillets and water in a medium pot, and bring to a boil over medium-high heat. Once boiling, reduce heat to medium; add salt, cilantro, and green onions.

With the flat side of a cleaver blade, crush the ginger on a chopping board, and add the ginger to the soup. Continue simmering until the fish is thoroughly cooked and the meat has turned white, about 7 minutes total. Remove ginger, and serve the soup with stir-fried dishes and steamed rice.

AUTUMN SOUP

Chinese vegetable soups tend to be more broth than vegetable, which is why I am always drawn to this heartier, chunkier soup with potatoes, acorn squash (substituted for Chinese pumpkin), and green beans. The textures, colors, and flavors of the vegetables bring to mind *autumn* — nothing could be more delightful on a crisp October day in Yunnan (or anywhere) than a bowl of this soup along with a meal of rice and stir-fry dishes.

Serves 4 to 6 in a family-style meal
Prep time: 20 minutes
Cooking time: 15 to 20 minutes

- 10 c. water
- 1 Tbsp vegetable bouillon powder
- half an acorn squash, washed, stem and seeds removed, and chopped in 1- to 1 1/2-inch cubes
- 2 small potatoes, peeled and chopped in 1- to 1 1/2-inch cubes
- 1/2 lb. green beans, washed, strings removed, and broken in 2- to 3-inch pieces
- 1 tsp salt

In a large pot bring the water to a boil over medium-high heat. Add the bouillon and stir until dissolved. Carefully add the squash, potatoes, and green beans, and reduce the heat to medium-low. Simmer the soup for 15 to 20 minutes, until the vegetables are soft but not mushy. Stir in salt before serving with steamed rice and other dishes as part of a family-style meal.

Shopping note:

If you wish to keep this recipe as a strictly vegetarian dish, be sure to purchase bouillon powder or cubes labeled "vegetarian vegetable."

Preparation note:

Good news — there's no need to remove the rind of an acorn squash before cooking or eating! The rind becomes tender as it cooks, so wash it well and enjoy your autumn soup.

MEAT AND FISH

FISH STEAMED WITH HERBS AND SPICES

My friend Lydia, of the Bulang ethnic group, taught me how to make this savory fish from her mother's recipe. Lydia's parents run a restaurant from their home on the banks of a river in a remote mountainous county in southwest Yunnan, and patrons drive for miles to sit and enjoy the view and eat their home-cooked village fare. Lydia and I made this steamed fish with two whole tilapia, fresh from the open air market, but sticking with the principle of simplicity, tilapia fillets work just as well. In my apartment in Yunnan we fashioned a make-shift steamer by crisscrossing a pair of chopsticks in the bottom of a pan to form a platform for a ceramic plate containing the fish and herbs. I've also made it in a bamboo steamer on top of a pot of water, and it can just as easily be done in a metal steamer — feel free to use whatever type of steamer you have on hand. See the **Preparation notes** below for more helpful tips.

Serves 6 as a main dish
Prep time: 5 minutes
Cooking time: about 20 minutes

- 1 24 oz. bag frozen tilapia fillets, thawed
- 2 Tbsp ginger in julienne slices
- 2 to 4 chilies, diced (use as many as you prefer, according to your taste)
- 2 Tbsp whole coriander seeds
- 1 1/2 tsp salt
- 1/3 c. cilantro, torn in pieces
- 3 green onions, cut in 1-inch strips
- several cabbage leaves

Place the tilapia in a large bowl. Add the ginger, chilies, coriander seeds, and salt; mix to coat the fish well.

Use the cabbage leaves to form a bed in the steamer; place the fish pieces in a layer on top of the cabbage. Arrange the cilantro and green onions on top of the fish. Place the steamer over a pot of water, and bring the water to a boil. Once steam begins to rise from the steamer, cook the fish for about 20 minutes, until it is thoroughly cooked and the meat has turned white. Serve with rice and stir-fried veggie dishes. **Corn Fried** with **Green and Red Peppers** and **Stir-fried Cabbage** work nicely with the fish.

Shopping notes:

For whole coriander seeds, try the bulk section of your supermarket, the spice section of the Hispanic food aisle, or the Asian market.

Preparation notes:

Regardless of the type of steamer you use, make sure the steamer tray fits tightly over the pot of water. You want to make sure that you let the water neither boil completely away, nor boil over. Fill the pot with enough water to ensure it won't boil away, and as an added layer of insurance, place a clean coin in the bottom of the pan — the coin should jingle as long as the water is boiling, letting you know the pot hasn't run dry. To keep the water from boiling over, start out at medium heat; after steam is steadily rising from the steamer, adjust the burner to medium-low heat, or just high enough to maintain a steady boil.

PORK AND PEPPERS

Pork and Peppers stands in my early Yunnan memories as a solid go-to dish to order when eating out with a group of friends. You never quite knew what you would get, whether the peppers would be spicy or sweet — it all depended on what the chef had on hand in the kitchen, but the result was always pleasing to the palate.

Serves 4 to 6 in a family-style meal
Prep time: 12 minutes
Cooking time: 8 minutes

- 2 Tbsp soy sauce (regular or gluten-free)
- 1 tsp sugar
- 1 tsp cornstarch
- 1 lb. pork, thinly sliced
- 2 green bell peppers, sliced
- 1/2 an onion, sliced
- 2 cloves garlic, minced
- 2 Tbsp oil

In a small bowl, combine the soy sauce, sugar, and cornstarch. Heat the oil in a wok over medium-high heat. Add the pork, peppers, onion, and garlic to the wok, and stir-fry until the pork is done and the peppers are tender-crisp, about 5 minutes. Pour the soy sauce mixture over the pork and vegetables, and stir-fry for another 2 to 3 minutes. Serve with rice.

PORK IN BANANA LEAF

In tropical southern Yunnan street vendors and fine restaurants alike feature the cooking method *bao kao*, or wrapping food in banana leaves and grilling it over coals. Pork, fish, and various vegetables are given similar treatment, flavored with herbs and spices and allowed to cook slowly. The technique can be easily duplicated by using foil and baking the ingredients in an oven, though banana leaves add a fun authentic touch if they are available.

Serves 6
Prep time: 20 minutes
Cooking time: 35 minutes

- 1 lb. ground pork
- 2 cloves garlic, minced
- 2 tsp ginger, minced
- 2 green onions, minced
- 3 tsp soy sauce (regular or gluten-free)
- 2 Tbsp cilantro, finely chopped
- 1 chili, minced
- salt to taste
- 2 banana leaves (optional)
- foil

Preheat the oven to 350 degrees.

Cut banana leaves and foil into 6 squares each, 8 inches by 8 inches.

Mix pork, garlic, ginger, green onions, soy sauce, cilantro, chili, and salt in a medium bowl. Divide the mixture into 6 portions.

If using banana leaves, first press a portion of the pork into the center of each of the 6 banana leaf squares. Wrap the edges of the banana leaf around the pork, and then wrap the foil around the leaf. If you're not using banana leaves, wrap the portions of pork directly in the foil squares. (Refer to photo for visual aid in wrapping the pork.)

Place the parcels on a baking tray and bake in oven for 35 minutes, or until meat is no longer pink. Serve warm with **Sticky Rice** or steamed rice.

41

Shopping note:

Banana leaves are generally available in Asian or Hispanic markets for a very reasonable price ($2 to $4 for a 1 lb. package). The leaves can be frozen and thawed when you're ready to use them.

HAM AND SOYBEANS WITH GOAT CHEESE

In Kunming and areas of Yunnan province with a large population of the Bai ethnic group, *ru bing* (a type of non-melting goat cheese) is a popular ingredient for stir-fried dishes. Thin squares of the cheese are added to pork, beans or peas, tomatoes, or other vegetables, or even fried or grilled and eaten alone. Ham is another Yunnan specialty in the world of Chinese cuisine. This dish of ham, soybeans, and goat cheese is one that I ate numerous times in Kunming restaurants, and I'm thrilled to find substitutes to replicate the dish in my American kitchen.

Serves 4 to 6 in a family-style meal
Prep time: 5 to 10 minutes
Cooking time: 8 minutes

- 5 oz. goat cheese (Chinese *ru bing* or Greek *halloumi*), sliced in small squares 1/4 inch thick
- 1 Tbsp oil
- 2 to 3 cloves garlic, minced
- 1 c. cured ham, sliced and cut in 1-inch pieces
- 1 c. shelled soybeans or green peas, frozen or fresh (If using fresh beans or peas, see **Preparation notes** below.)

Without adding oil, heat a wok on medium-high heat; add the cheese squares and allow to lightly brown on both sides, about 1 to 2 minutes per side. The cheese will have been soaked in brine and will release water as it fries, making oil unnecessary. Remove the browned cheese and set aside.

Add the oil to the hot wok, and fry the garlic and ham until browned, about 2 minutes. Add the softened soybeans or peas, and stir-fry for another 2 minutes. Add the browned cheese back to the wok and gently stir-fry to warm through. Serve hot with rice and other stir-fry dishes.

Shopping notes:

If you're fortunate enough to live in China and have access to Yunnan ham and *ru bing*, you'll want to stick with those two as the most authentic ingredients for this dish. If you're cooking in a Western context, you can substitute cured ham and the Greek cheese *halloumi*. Ham and *halloumi* are both high in sodium, so no need to add salt to this dish.

Preparation note:

If you're using fresh soybeans or peas, you will need to soften them before stir-frying with the ham and cheese. Steam or boil the shelled beans or peas for 5 minutes; drain water before stir-frying.

VEGETABLES AND FRUITS

PICKLED TURNIPS

Pickled or preserved vegetables of all types are a must as a condiment on the side of a true Yunnanese meal. Greens, roots, chopped green beans — sour, salty, and spicy. A spoonful or two of Pickled Greens can also liven up a dish of **Fried Rice** or stir-fried veggies (see **Crispy Beans with Pickled Greens**) and give it a distinctive flavor of Yunnan. **Pickled Turnips** feature prominently in the tang of **Pork-and-Turnip Rice**.

The ideal way to make these two types of pickled vegetables would be to use turnips and their greens from your own garden or purchased together from a farmers market, but any type of greens will work just fine.

- 2 turnips (about 1 1/4 lb.), chopped
- 2 cloves garlic, peeled, whole
- 2 chilies (red or green), stems removed and sliced diagonally into 3 to 4 pieces each
- 2 c. water
- 1 c. white vinegar
- 1 Tbsp salt
- 2 Tbsp sugar

Wash and dry 1 quart jar and lid, or 2 pint jars and lids. Wash, peel, and chop the turnips into small pieces. Layer the turnips, garlic cloves, and chili slices in the jar(s) until full. If you use 2 pint jars, make sure each jar has 1 clove of garlic and an equal amount of chili slices.

In a small saucepan, combine the water, vinegar, salt, and sugar, and bring to a boil, stirring to dissolve the sugar and salt. Allow to cool 2 to 3 minutes, and pour the liquid into the jar(s) until all the turnip pieces are covered. Once the liquid has cooled to room temperature, cover the jar(s) with the lid(s) and refrigerate until use.

Preparation note:

Pouring the hot liquid directly from the saucepan into the jars can be messy. Use a ladle and funnel to prevent spills.

PICKLED GREENS

- 1 lb. greens (collard, mustard, turnip, whatever suits your fancy), stems removed and leaves coarsely chopped
- 2 cloves garlic, peeled, whole
- 2 chilies (red or green), stems removed and sliced diagonally into 3 to 4 pieces each
- 2 c. water
- 1 c. white vinegar
- 1 Tbsp salt
- 2 Tbsp sugar

Wash and dry 1 quart jar and lid, or 2 pint jars and lids. Layer the chopped greens, garlic cloves, and chili slices in the jar(s) until full, packing down the greens as necessary. If you use 2 pint jars, make sure each jar has 1 clove of garlic and an equal amount of chili slices.

In a small saucepan, combine the water, vinegar, salt, and sugar, and bring to a boil, stirring to dissolve the sugar and salt. Allow to cool 2 to 3 minutes, and pour the liquid into the jar(s) until all the chopped greens are covered. Once the liquid has cooled to room temperature, cover the jar(s) with the lid(s) and refrigerate until use.

Preparation note:

Pouring the hot liquid directly from the saucepan into the jars can be messy. Use a ladle and funnel to prevent spills.

CUCUMBER SALAD

This salad with cucumbers, tomatoes, and red onion is a refreshing, light dish served at both Dai restaurants and street restaurants in southern Yunnan. On a hot, tropical day nothing beats a meal with a cool Cucumber Salad and a glass of **Xishuangbanna Limeade**.

Serves: 4 to 6 in a family-style meal
Prep time: 10 minutes

- 2 cucumbers (about 3 to 4 c.), peeled, seeds removed, cut in 3/4-inch cubes
- 2 medium tomatoes (about 3 c.), cut in 3/4-inch cubes
- half a red onion (about 1 c.), thinly sliced
- 1/4 c. cilantro, finely chopped
- 2 Tbsp soy sauce (regular or gluten-free)
- 2 Tbsp rice vinegar
- 1 to 2 cloves garlic, minced
- 1/2 tsp salt
- 2 tsp sugar
- half a chili (about 2 Tbsp), finely chopped (optional)

In a large bowl mix the cucumber, tomato, onion, and cilantro.

In a small bowl mix the soy sauce, vinegar, garlic, salt, sugar, and chili (optional). Pour over the cucumber mixture, and toss the vegetables to coat well.

Shopping note:
Some specialty vinegars may contain gluten. If you are on a gluten-free diet, check the label on the rice vinegar to make sure you are purchasing a gluten-free variety.

49

GREEN BEANS WITH GARLIC

Even if the rest of your meal has a non-Asian flavor, this variation on fresh green beans can liven up your dinner and provide a needed boost to convince your pickiest eaters that veggies aren't boring.

Serves: 4 to 6 in a family-style meal
Prep time: 15 minutes
Cooking time: 12 minutes

- 1 lb. fresh green beans
- 4 tsp soy sauce (regular or gluten-free)
- 1 tsp sugar
- 1 Tbsp water
- 1 1/2 Tbsp oil
- 3 cloves garlic, minced
- 1 Tbsp fresh ginger, minced

Wash the green beans, and remove the ends and any strings; cut diagonally into 2-inch or longer pieces.

Stir together the soy sauce, sugar, and water in a small bowl; set aside.

Heat the oil in a wok over medium-high heat. When the oil is hot, add the garlic, ginger, and green beans; stir-fry for 1 minute. Stir in the liquid mixture. Reduce the heat to medium, cover the wok, and cook until the beans are tender-crisp, about 6 to 7 minutes.

Uncover the wok, and increase the burner to high heat. Boil and stir until almost all the liquid has evaporated, about 1 to 3 minutes. Serve while hot.

STIR FRIED CABBAGE

So basic and so good. As it does in the **Fried Rice** recipe, the dried red pepper gives this dish its distinctly Yunnan flavor.

Serves 4 to 6 in a family-style meal
Prep time: 10 minutes
Cooking time: 5 minutes

- 1 Tbsp oil
- 2 cloves garlic, minced
- 1 dried red pepper, sliced in half lengthwise, seeds removed
- half a head of cabbage (green, Napa, or Savoy) (about 4 c.), shredded
- 1 Tbsp soy sauce (regular or gluten-free)
- 1 Tbsp cooking wine (or substitute water)

Heat the oil in a wok over medium-high heat. When the oil is hot, add the garlic and dried pepper; stir-fry for 1 minute to brown the garlic. Add the cabbage and stir to mix well with oil and garlic. Cover the wok and cook for 1 minute. Remove the lid, and add the soy sauce and cooking wine. Cook for another 2 minutes, until the cabbage is tender. Serve warm with steamed rice and other dishes.

Shopping note:

If your grocery store doesn't have dried red peppers in their Asian food section, check the Hispanic food aisle for whole dried Japanese peppers (*chili japones entero*).

Preparation note:

Almost any type of green, leafy vegetable can be substituted for cabbage in this recipe. The possibilities are only limited by your taste preference and the vegetables you have on hand.

CORN FRIED WITH GREEN AND RED PEPPERS

Typically I go for fresh ingredients over frozen, but depending on the time of year fresh corn might not be the best option for this colorful dish. If you're satisfied with flavor over looks, use fresh corn when available, even if it's lighter in color. If you want the full vibrancy of bright yellow, green, and red, stick with frozen kernels for consistency's sake. Either way, this simple dish makes a tasty, eye-catching side.

Serves 4 to 6 in a family-style meal
Prep time: 10 minutes (frozen corn) or 20 to 25 minutes (fresh corn)
Cooking time: 5 to 7 minutes

- 1 Tbsp oil
- 1 clove garlic, minced
- 3 to 4 cobs of fresh corn, cooked and kernels removed from the cob, or 2 c. frozen corn (thawed)
- 1/2 c. green bell pepper, chopped
- 1/2 c. red bell pepper, chopped
- salt to taste

Heat the oil in a wok over medium-high heat. Add the garlic and stir for 1 minute. Add the corn and peppers, cooking until the peppers are tender-crisp, about 4 to 5 minutes. Stir in salt to taste. Serve while hot.

Preparation note:

If using fresh cobs of corn, remove the husks and strings, and add the cobs to a large pot of boiling water. Cover the pot, return to a boil, and cook for 5 minutes. Remove the corn from the water, and allow to cool to the touch. Cut the kernels from the cob with a knife.

CRISPY BEANS WITH PICKLED GREENS

A Kunming favorite — try this dish with **Pork and Peppers**, **Grandma Potatoes**, and steamed rice.

Serves 4 to 6 in a family-style meal
Prep time: 5 minutes
Cooking time: 5 minutes

- 1/3 c. flour
- 1 tsp salt
- 1 tsp chili powder
- 1 tsp garlic powder
- 1 15.5 oz. can kidney beans, drained and rinsed
- 3 Tbsp vegetable oil
- 2 Tbsp **Pickled Greens**

In a medium bowl mix the flour, salt, chili powder, and garlic powder. Dredge the kidney beans in the flour mixture, lightly coating each individual bean and removing the beans from the flour mixture to a separate plate.

Heat the oil in a wok over medium-high heat. When the oil is hot, add the flour-coated beans and fry for 3 to 4 minutes until crispy, occasionally giving the beans a gentle stir. Remove the beans to a paper-towel-lined plate. Add the **Pickled Greens** to the wok and stir-fry for about 20 to 30 seconds, just until the greens are heated through. Return the beans to the wok, and stir just until mixed well with the Pickled Greens. Serve warm with steamed rice and other dishes.

TOFU WITH GREEN ONIONS AND TOMATO

Serves 4 to 6 in a family-style meal
Prep time: 5 minutes
Cooking time: 5 minutes

- 1 Tbsp oil
- 1 clove garlic, minced
- 1 16 oz. package firm or extra firm tofu, cut in thin slices
- 2 small tomatoes, cut in 1-inch sections
- 3 green onions, cut in 1 1/2-inch strips
- 1/2 tsp salt

Heat the oil in a wok over medium-high heat. When the oil is hot, add the garlic and fry for 1 minute. Add the tofu and stir gently to fry for 1 minute, being careful not to break up the tofu slices. Add the tomato slices and stir-fry for 2 minutes. Add the green onion and fry for 1 minute. Sprinkle the dish with salt and give the dish one last stir to season throughout. Serve with steamed rice and other stir-fry dishes.

GRANDMA POTATOES

Some people say the dish gets its name because these potatoes are "the way grandma makes them." Others in Kunming say the name comes from the fact that an old lady with no teeth can easily eat these soft potatoes. Either way, these potatoes are a nice side to other Kunming-style stir-fry dishes, such as **Crispy Beans with Pickled Greens**, **Stir-fried Cabbage**, or **Ham and Soybeans with Goat Cheese**.

Serves 4 to 6 in a family-style meal
Prep time: 10 minutes
Cooking time: 25 minutes

- 6 c. water
- 3 medium potatoes, peeled and chopped in 1-inch chunks
- 1 Tbsp oil
- 2 green onions, chopped in 1/2-inch strips
- 2 tsp chili powder
- 1 tsp salt

Bring the water to a boil in a medium pot, and add the potatoes. Boil for 15 to 20 minutes, until potatoes are tender. Drain the water and place the potatoes on a cutting board. Chop the potatoes roughly into smaller chunks.

Heat the oil in a wok over medium-high heat, and add the green onions and chili powder. Stir-fry for 1 minute. Add the potatoes and salt, and mix to coat the potatoes well with the oil and onions. Continue breaking up and mashing the potatoes with your cooking utensil, frying for another 2 to 3 minutes. Serve with steamed rice and other family-style dishes.

CRISPY YUNNAN HASHBROWNS

Serves 4 to 6 in a family style meal
Prep time: 15 minutes
Cooking time: 15 minutes

- 2 medium potatoes (about 1 1/2 c.), cut in thin matchstick-sized pieces
- 1 tsp salt
- 1 dried red pepper, sliced in half lengthwise, seeds removed
- 3 Tbsp oil

In a medium bowl, toss together the potatoes, salt, and dried pepper. Heat the oil in a wok over medium-high heat. Pour the potato mixture into the wok, and use your spatula to spread the potatoes into a thin layer across the surface of the wok, forming one large cake of hashbrowns. Cook the potatoes for 7 to 8 minutes, adjusting the temperature to achieve golden brown and crispy hashbrowns. If using a gas stove, you may need to move the wok every 30 seconds or so to ensure that every area of the hashbrown surface is cooking evenly.

Once the bottom of the potatoes has begun to brown, use your spatula to flip the entire hashbrown like a pancake. Continue cooking the opposite side another 5 to 7 minutes, until the potatoes are completely tender on the inside with a crispy golden outside. Move the hashbrown to a plate covered with a paper towel to soak up excess oil. Cut the hashbrown into triangles like a pizza, and serve with steamed rice and stir-fried dishes.

Shopping note:

If your grocery store doesn't have dried red peppers in their Asian food section, check the Hispanic food aisle for whole dried Japanese peppers (*chili japones entero*).

Preparation note:

The thinner you cut the potatoes, the better. If your matchsticks are too thick, the outside of the hashbrowns will be oily and soggy, not golden and crispy.

SPICY SWEET EGGPLANT

Originally a Sichuan (Szechuan) dish, this Spicy Sweet Eggplant is now found all throughout Southwest China and is particularly popular in Yunnan, a province as famous as Sichuan for its peppery cuisine. The Chinese name for the dish (*yu xiang qie zi*) is often translated "fish fragrant eggplant," although the dish itself has nothing to do with fish. I prefer the descriptor "spicy sweet" and hope you enjoy the flavors of this delightful eggplant as much as I do.

Serves 4 to 6 in a family-style meal
Prep time: 15 minutes
Cooking time: 6 minutes

- 2 tsp cornstarch
- 1 Tbsp sugar
- 2 Tbsp rice vinegar
- 2 Tbsp soy sauce (regular or gluten-free)
- 4 Tbsp water
- 2 Tbsp oil
- 1 1/4 to 1 1/2 lbs. eggplant (about 1 large eggplant or 3 Japanese eggplants), cut in 1 1/2-inch cubes
- 2 cloves garlic, minced
- 2 tsp ginger, minced
- 2 dried red peppers, sliced in half lengthwise, seeds removed
- 5 green onions, cut in 2-inch strips

In a small bowl, mix cornstarch, sugar, vinegar, soy sauce, and water; set aside.

Heat the oil in a wok over medium-high heat. When the oil is hot, add the eggplant cubes and stir-fry for 2 minutes. Add the garlic, ginger, dried red peppers, and green onions, and stir-fry for 1 minute.

Stir the sauce ingredients briefly to mix the sugar and cornstarch that will have settled on the bottom of the bowl. Pour the sauce mixture over the eggplant in the wok, and stir to coat the eggplant thoroughly. Continue cooking until the eggplant is soft (but not mushy) and the sauce begins to thicken, about 3 to 4 minutes. Serve warm with steamed rice and other dishes.

Shopping notes:

If your grocery store doesn't have dried red peppers in their Asian food section, check the Hispanic food aisle for whole dried Japanese peppers (*chili japones entero*).

Some specialty vinegars may contain gluten. If you are on a gluten-free diet, check the label on the rice vinegar to make sure you are purchasing a gluten-free variety.

ROASTED EGGPLANT

Roasted Eggplant is often served in southern Yunnan at outdoor *shao kao* (barbecue grill) restaurants or street vendors, and it nicely accompanies the **Roasted Tomato Dip** or **Pork in Banana Leaf**.

Serves 4
Prep time: 10 minutes
Cooking time: 40 minutes

• 1 large eggplant or 2 Japanese eggplants, washed and sliced in half lengthwise
• 2 cloves garlic, minced
• 2 green onions, chopped
• 1/4 c. cilantro, finely chopped
• 1 chili, seeded and minced (optional)
• 2 tsp soy sauce (regular or gluten-free)
• 1/2 tsp salt

Preheat oven to 400 degrees.

Line a baking sheet with foil, and place eggplant halves on the sheet with the peel side facing up. Bake for 40 minutes, until very tender. Allow the eggplant to cool to the touch.

Remove and discard the peel. Place the eggplant sections in a medium bowl. Add garlic, green onions, cilantro, chili, soy sauce, and salt to the eggplant and mix well. Serve with **Sticky Rice** or steamed rice and other dishes.

ROASTED TOMATO DIP

Along with **Roasted Eggplant**, this Roasted Tomato Dip is a favorite at *shao kao* (barbecue grill) restaurants of the Dai people in the Xishuangbanna area of southern Yunnan. The dip is often available from vendors in outdoor markets and is mixed using a mortar and pestle. I would satisfy my Mexican food craving by taking it home to eat with tortilla chips, but it is typically eaten at Dai meals using chunks of cucumber, string beans, other local vegetables, or balls of **Sticky Rice** as dippers.

Serves 4
Prep time: 10 minutes
Cooking time: 25 to 30 minutes

• 3 to 4 medium tomatoes, stems removed, cut in quarters
• 4 cloves garlic, minced
• 1/3 c. cilantro, finely chopped
• 1 to 2 chilies, finely chopped (optional)
• 2 tsp soy sauce (regular or gluten-free)
• chunks of cucumber, string beans, cabbage, or other vegetables for dipping

Preheat oven to 350 degrees.

Line a baking sheet with foil, and place tomato quarters on the sheet with the peel side facing up. Bake for 25 to 30 minutes, until very tender. Allow to cool to the touch and remove the peels.

In a medium bowl mix the roasted tomato sections, garlic, cilantro, chilies (optional), and soy sauce until well blended, using the edge of your spoon to break up and mash the tomato sections. Serve with **Sticky Rice** and other dishes.

Preparation Note:
Dai cooks typically leave the peel on the tomatoes in this dish, but if you prefer, the peels can easily be removed after the tomatoes have been roasted.

Fried Bananas

A popular dessert among backpackers in Southeast Asia, Fried Bananas became a comfort food for me when eating out with both Chinese and Western friends in Kunming — the batter reminds me of funnel cake from home, but when it's combined with the cooked banana this dish is pure Southeast Asia.

Serves 4
Prep time: 5 minutes
Cooking time: 5 minutes per batch of bananas

- 3/4 c. flour
- 2 Tbsp sugar
- pinch of salt
- pinch of baking soda
- 1/2 c. milk
- 1 egg, beaten
- 2 bananas, peeled and sliced in 1/2-inch slices
- enough oil to coat the bottom of a small frying pan in a 3/4 inch layer
- 2 tsp powdered sugar

In a small bowl combine flour, sugar, salt, and baking soda. Add the milk and beaten egg and whisk to form a batter the consistency of pancake batter. Dredge the banana pieces in the batter.

In a frying pan heat the oil until a drop of water sizzles when dropped in the oil. Using a slotted spoon, dip the banana pieces out of the batter and place gently in the oil. Allow the banana pieces to fry until golden brown and puffy, about 5 minutes; turn once, if necessary, to brown the opposite side. Carefully scoop the bananas out of the frying pan and place on a paper-towel-lined plate to drain of excess oil. Immediately transfer to a serving dish, being careful to not let the bananas stick to the paper towel. Sprinkle with powdered sugar, and serve as a dessert or as a side dish.

Shopping note:

Unlike dishes made from green plantains in Central America, be sure to use ripe bananas to make these Southeast Asian-style Fried Bananas.

Preparation note:

My 8-inch cast iron skillet works perfectly for frying the bananas in three batches, making the best use of the smallest amount of oil.

XISHUANGBANNA LIMEADE

Countless restaurants and roadside food stalls in Xishuangbanna serve limeade — limes are a key ingredient in many dishes made by the Dai people of the region. This icy beverage is refreshing year-round, but even more so in the hottest part of the year in the tropics. The blended version featured here is based on the recipe of the best-selling drink I enjoyed often at the Mountain Cafe while living in Jinghong.

Serves 4 to 6
Prep time: 30 minutes if you squeeze fresh limes; 5 minutes if using bottled lime juice
Cooking time: 5 minutes

- 1 1/2 c. sugar
- 1 1/2 c. water
- 4 c. ice cubes
- 1 to 1 1/4 c. lime juice (bottled or fresh-squeezed)

In a medium pan stir together sugar and water over medium-high heat. Bring to a boil; reduce heat and let simmer about 5 minutes, stirring constantly, until the mixture reaches a syrupy consistency. Remove from heat; cool to room temperature.

Place ice cubes in blender, and pour in lime juice and sugar water over the ice. Blend about 10 seconds until the limeade reaches a slushy consistency. Pour into glasses and serve immediately.

Preparation note:
This limeade works equally well with bottled or fresh lime juice. You will need 8 to 12 limes for about 1 c. juice, depending on the size of the limes.

ACKNOWLEDGEMENTS

Many of the people I want to thank for their help with this book will never see it. I owe deep gratitude to my friends in Yunnan and to numerous restaurant cooks whose names I do not know. In particular I wish to thank Lydia for sharing countless meals with me in my apartment and at her village home. I also would like to thank Lydia's Meh (mother) and the other Bulang, Dai, and Han ladies who showed me how to prepare the most delicious of meals in the simplest of kitchens.

Friends and family take a risk when agreeing to taste test recipes during the writing phase. It sounds like an enjoyable job – until they have to try a recipe that is in the far-from-perfect stage. Thank you to those who were willing to chance these recipes in all the stages of this cookbook, particularly Jane and Andy Cassinelli, Laura and Abner Solano, and others in my small group at Quinault. My parents, Bob and Linda Henderson, also did their fair share of taste-testing, and my mom did more than her share of proofreading and editing. As always, she gently corrected my mistakes, and any remaining blunders are my own fault.

The greatest burden of the writing and testing of this cookbook fell to Stephen, my boyfriend and fiancé at the time of writing, now my husband at publication. Whether he married me because of or in spite of my endeavors in the kitchen, only he can say. But any man who is willing to try out a tofu dish on the first evening I cook for him, well, that's the man for me. Thank you, Stephen, for being a good sport and for all your love and encouragement. Here's to an infinite number of meals together in the future.

ABOUT THE AUTHOR

Rebecca D. Henderson spent ten years living in Yunnan, China, near the border of Burma and Laos, where she worked as an English teacher, translator, amateur linguist, semi-professional truck driver, and barista, among many other jobs. She now lives and writes in Texas with her husband and four step-sons. She also cooks, runs, gardens, and hunts for buried treasure at thrift stores and garage sales.

www.rebeccadiann.com
www.twitter.com/rebeccadiann
www.facebook.com/pages/Simply-Yunnan

Also by Rebecca D. Henderson:

From the Tea Village
a Young Adult novel

"A Separate Escape"
in *That Mad Game: Growing up in a war-zone*

Please enjoy the following sample chapter from
From the Tea Village

CHAPTER 1

A QUESTION FOR BO

I T WAS JIANG LAO SHI'S idea for me to go to town for middle school. Meh and Bo listened to him and followed his words the same way they had with my earlier teachers. They respected him because he was my teacher and because he treated the parents from the villages kindly.

"Not every town person wants to help village students, Ye Sun," Meh said, calling me by my Bulang name. "But this teacher, he is different."

Jiang Lao Shi—he was both my math teacher and my head teacher, or *lao shi,* my last year at Mang Kai Primary School. By that year we knew him well. We knew just how much we needed to do in class during the week so that he would reward us with a trip down to the river to swim on Friday afternoon.

On a market day in spring before we were to finish sixth grade, Jiang Lao Shi had bell duty. All across China, even in our corner of far-away Yunnan, the morning bell rings early to awaken both students and teachers. 6:30. Two hours before daylight during the winter months.

There were no alarm clocks at Mang Kai Primary School. Each morning before classes, before breakfast, before morning exercises, the teacher on duty struck metal on metal to wake us up. The teacher struck the bell to end each class period, to send us to lunch, to call us back from our midday nap, to send us to dinner, and then to bring us to evening reviews.

For three years at Mang Kai Primary School, I was our class leader and helped the teachers with small jobs around the school grounds. Jiang Lao Shi asked me to take over bell duty for him because he knew I owned a watch. Meh bought it for me when I came to the school at Mang Kai. I didn't need it before then—a watch is unnecessary in a Bulang village, where the schedule runs according to the sun, not by hours and minutes.

Towards the end of the last class period on that market day in spring, I kept an eye on my watch until the right moment and slipped out to the courtyard to strike the bell. On my way out the door, Jiang Lao Shi nodded at me from the chalkboard. The whole school waited for me—if I didn't go out to ring that bell, everyone would be stuck in an endless lesson.

At the sound of the clanging, students in the twelve classrooms of our school slammed shut their textbooks, scraped their wooden chair legs on the concrete floor, and rushed into the courtyard to be the first in line at the dining hall. Gao Song waited for me by the climbing bougainvillea in full bloom on the side of the two-story classroom building. She plucked a purple flower from the bush and tucked it behind her ear.

"Let's take our rice to Jiang Lao Shi's place today," she said and took my hand in hers. "Jiang Su Yin said she would wait for us there."

The block of one-story teachers' apartments stretched one room after another in a straight chain, a simple concrete building with no insulation to keep out the winter chill, same as the students' dorm where Gao Song and I slept. Jiang Lao Shi lived with his wife and niece in two rooms in the middle of the apartment block, one room for the adults and another that served as both sitting room and bedroom for our classmate, Jiang Su Yin.

We took our rice bowls from the dining hall to eat crowded around a low table in their sitting room. Gao Song and I ate our rice and stir-fried vegetables purchased with meal tickets from the school dining hall, and Jiang Lao Shi's wife dished into their family's bowls the meal she cooked over a hot plate outside their apartment door.

"You need to eat more," she said and scooped fried bits of pork into our bowls, mindful that neither Gao Song nor I had meat from the dining hall.

After dinner, while Jiang Lao Shi and his wife sat on short stools on the sidewalk outside their apartment, talking to the teachers from two doors down, my friends and I washed the dishes in the water basin at the end of the apartment row. The evening breeze of spring brushed my hair against my neck. We slopped the water over the edges of the concrete basin onto our shoes and carried the dripping dishes to stack on the table to dry.

The nearby rumbling of a *tuo la ji* engine broke through the sound of our classmates' voices in the school courtyard. The tractor engine coughed and idled for a moment before the driver cut it off. Several times a day we heard *tuo la ji* chugging their way up the road between town and the outlying villages, their wooden beds loaded with passengers piled on top of crates and rice sacks and baskets. The drivers of these *tuo la ji* did decent business, earning a couple of *yuan* from each person who rode with them or transported goods, whether vegetables, tea, or rice from their fields to be sold in the market or the merchandise they purchased in town to be used back home in the village.

My father drove his own *tuo la ji* to town every five days on market day, taking a load of people and goods to market in the morning and carrying them home in the evening. Market day was also a time for Bo to stock up on the items Meh needed for the little shop she ran from the front window of our house. Noodles, crackers, small packets of shampoo, cigarettes, bottles of water and cola and alcohol, all purchased at the market in town and resold to folks from the outlying villages.

Late this afternoon, as he usually did on market day, Bo stopped at the gate to the Mang Kai school compound for a quick visit with my teacher while his passengers waited. The passengers would rather go home straight away, but that's just the way it is in the mountains of Yunnan—the driver determines the schedule.

Bo rounded the corner of the teachers' building as Gao Song, Jiang Su Yin, and I were gathering our notebooks to go back to the classroom for evening reviews. I smiled when I saw him, a bag of steamed bread and a jar of Meh's pickled turnips in his hands. He nodded to me, but moved directly to where Jiang Lao Shi and his wife sat on their stools leaning against the apartment wall.

Jiang Lao Shi stood up to greet my father. "Mr. Li, good to see you."

"*Lao shi*, good evening," Bo said. "On my way home from the market—my wife sent this for your family to enjoy." He extended the jar of pickled turnips to my teacher, who began the customary show of manners and appreciation.

Jiang Lao Shi motioned with his hands in an effort not to accept the jar. "*Wah*, Mr. Li, this is too much. We are still enjoying the chilies you brought us last time."

"No, no, you must take them," Bo said. "Share them with the other teachers."

"You're too kind, too kind. You really must stop bringing these treats to us." The truth was, Meh's pickles were the best around and everyone knew it. Jiang Lao Shi wanted no such thing as for her to stop sending them.

My teacher and my father continued their back and forth of pleasantries and formalities, asking after each other's health, my mother back at home, and my grades. I pulled Gao Song's sleeve to have her wait before leaving for evening reviews. I knew Bo wouldn't say much to me on this visit—convention demanded that he pay the most attention to my teacher, the person with higher status—but I knew that the bag of steamed bread he still held in his hand was for me.

"We'll wait," Jiang Su Yin whispered. She and Gao Song and I huddled together to the side of the porch, close enough to hear clearly but far enough to show respect for the adults.

Jiang Lao Shi offered Bo a cigarette, which he tucked behind his ear for later. "Sit for a cup of tea, will you?" Jiang Lao Shi said and pulled up a stool for Bo.

"*Xie xie, xie xie,* thank you, but I can't," Bo said. "My passengers are waiting." He stepped back and waved a hand to refuse the seat.

"Before you leave, I have something I've wanted to discuss with you," Jiang Lao Shi said and glanced towards me.

My face heated up. Why did my teacher need to talk about me with my father? As head teacher for my class, Class A of Grade Six at Mang Kai Primary School, Jiang Lao Shi handled all our grades, made sure we paid our fees, and helped us if we had any trouble with money or with a family emergency at home. If we needed a doctor, if we needed someone to talk to while our mothers and fathers were miles away and busy in the fields, we went to Jiang Lao Shi.

And he was the teacher who reported back to our parents on our grades, our behavior in class, any problems we had that they might not know of while we were boarding at school.

Jiang Su Yin tucked her arm through mine to pull me closer to her side, and we waited to hear what Jiang Lao Shi would say.

"The entrance exam for middle school will take place in two months. Your daughter would do well to take it." I looked up to see him nodding towards me and my two friends. "All three of them have a good chance of getting spots at the middle school in town."

Bo kicked idly at the dirt on the pavement with his heel, his hands in his pockets. He looked away from Jiang Lao Shi, across the school yard to the students filing into the kitchen building to fill their empty rice bowls.

"Her mother could use her help back home in the tea fields," Bo said. "It's hard enough to send her and our younger two here to Mang Kai village for school—I don't know how we'll find the money to pay for her to live and eat in town." He drew a deep breath and continued. "You think she could do well on the exam?"

"Her math scores are the highest in her grade. The highest I've ever seen, actually. She will need to improve her spoken Mandarin and her character writing." Jiang Lao Shi's voice was stern with a comment intended as much for me as for Bo. "But I think she could do well enough to pass the exam."

Jiang Lao Shi caught my eye again. "I would hate to see her leave school at this point," he said.

I blushed again to hear Jiang Lao Shi speak well of me to Bo in front of my friends. The heat flowed from my cheeks to the tips of my ears, and my stomach tightened at the thought of going to middle school. No one from Gai Lan village went to school beyond the sixth grade at Mang Kai. Bo came to school in Mang Kai when he was young, but Meh only went through third grade at the one-room school back home in Gai Lan. The Bulang from our mountains had rice fields to plow for food and tea leaves to pick for cash, and all the work was done by hand and by the sweat of hard labor. Reading and math and learning history was a luxury for the Han Chinese, or maybe for more affluent ethnic minority groups like the Dai—but not for the Bulang.

Bo was silent, his face still, his gaze fixed on the kitchen building. I couldn't speak to him, not in front of Jiang Lao Shi and his wife, though they were planning my future for me. I had to be quiet and wait. And it was just as well, for at that moment the idea of going to middle school in town was too new for me to know how to respond.

Without looking to me, Bo turned to Jiang Lao Shi. "Maybe she could do well enough," he said. "Let her take the exam, but I can't say what will happen after this school year is over."

At last Bo acknowledged my presence and held out the bag of steamed bread towards me. "Ye Sun," he said, "share these with your sister and brother."

I came forward and took the bag from him. "*Xie xie*, Bo," I said. He met my eyes, and I saw pride in his look.

"My passengers must be wondering if we're ever going to head home," Bo said, and he left Jiang Lao Shi's apartment for his *tuo la ji*. The conversation was over as quickly as Jiang Lao Shi had begun it.